FOR DAVID

This is the story of three kings of Israel : Saul, who was often sad and did not trust enough in God ; David, a brave and sensible man who knew that he could govern his people well only with the help of God ; and Solomon, David's son, who built the Temple in Jerusalem and forgot God.

Nihil obstat: Francis Bartlett, Censor
Imprimatur: ✠ Patrick Casey, Vicar General. Westminster, 15 May 1967

First published 1967 by Burns & Oates Ltd, 25 Ashley Place, London S.W. 1

THE BIBLE FOR CHILDREN
by HAMISH SWANSTON
VOLUME FOUR

David and his Son

Pictures by EMILE PROBST

LONDON · BURNS & OATES

Once the people of Israel had crossed into Canaan they set about making a home for themselves. The men of Canaan did not care for them at all, and, led by the warrior Philistines, they made every effort to push the Israelites out of the land.

Surrounded by their enemies, the men of Israel talked with Samuel, their old prophet. They realized that if they were to keep the land that God had given them they would have to be more organized. They told Samuel to ask God for a king to lead them.

God gave them a king. His name was Saul. He was young and handsome and tall. The whole people stood watching as Samuel poured oil on Saul's head to show that he was the new king.

Saul was not a very good king. He was too impatient and moody. Samuel liked the king but he saw that he was not really the man to lead the people of God. The old prophet set out to look for another man to take Saul's place. In the hill country he met David, a young shepherd. As soon as he saw him Samuel knew that this shepherd boy was chosen by God to be king of his people after Saul. While David's family looked on Samuel poured oil on the boy's head.

Saul knew nothing about all this.

The men of Israel were at war with the Philistines. In his tent Saul, the king of the Israelites, waited for the attack.

Saul was an unhappy man. It seemed to him that he could never do anything right. His soldiers did not care for these dismal thoughts. They brought David to the king. David sang songs and played his harp and Saul became much better tempered.

Saul kept David in the camp to sing for him whenever he felt sad.

One morning the Israelite soldiers were woken up by the loud shouts of a rough, tough Philistine. He was very tall and very strong and very fierce. His name was Goliath. "Come out," he roared to the Israelites, "and find a man to fight me. If I kill him you shall be our slaves; if he kills me we will serve you." The Israelites trembled. They did not think that anyone in their camp could defeat a man like Goliath.

When David heard Goliath shout he said to Saul: "I will go out and fight that Philistine bully." Saul did not think this at all a good idea. "Goliath is much too big for you. He would kill you and we would all become slaves for the Philistines," Saul said. "No, no," laughed David; "have a little more faith in God and do not be afraid."

Saul saw that it was no use trying to persuade David to stay in the tent.

"At least," the king said, "wear my own royal armour to protect yourself against this ruffian." David put on the king's armour but it was so heavy that he could not walk in it. David took off the armour and stepped out to meet Goliath with only his catapult and five smooth stones from the river bed. David trusted God and knew that he had nothing to fear from a Philistine boaster who cared nothing for God.

Goliath laughed and shouted horrible oaths as David walked towards him. David slung a stone in his catapult, aimed, and the whirling stone struck Goliath in the forehead. The terrible man fell headlong and the Philistines ran away.

Everybody in the Israelite camp was very pleased with David. They made up a song about his defeat of Goliath. David chased the Philistines over the hills and far away. When he came back to the camp the men cheered and the girls stopped work at the cooking pots and sang their song of David's victory.

All this was rather too much for Saul. The king was not pleased that David was more popular than he was. When David came to the king's tent to play his harp Saul took up a spear and lunged at David. He missed.

David ran out of the tent and did not come to play his harp again.

Saul forgot the times when David playing on his harp had driven away his sadness; he forgot the times when David leading the Israelite troops had driven away his enemies; he forgot everything.   He was very jealous.

Saul said to his soldiers: "Find David and kill him.   He is my enemy."   The soldiers looked at each other in great surprise but they did not dare to oppose the angry king. Only Jonathan, the king's son, asked: "Why have you suddenly turned against David, father?"

"He is a traitor.   He would steal the crown and wear it himself."

Jonathan would not believe that his friend was a traitor.   "How do you know all this?" he asked his father.

"You are a fool," Saul shouted.   "Any more of this and I'll kill you too," he added, fingering his spear.

Jonathan left the king's tent and went to look for David.   He told David that he must hurry away.   The two friends were sad at parting.   They promised that they would be friends whatever happened.

David hurried away from Saul's camp and went to live in the hill country. Because he was such a fine leader many men came to join him. Soon he had a large band of comrades.

When Saul heard of David's escape he was very angry. The king set out with his troops into the hill country to catch David. David was too quick for him. He knew how to hide in caves and run along the valleys when Saul was searching the other side of the hill. He was never caught.

The Philistines learnt that Saul was busy chasing David in the hills. They came up behind him and attacked the Israelite army. Saul had to turn round and fight them. Life was very hectic for Saul.

The king grew old and tired and the Philistines kept on attacking him just when he thought he could have a little peace. At last the enemy warriors surrounded Saul and his son Jonathan on a hill-top and killed them. The army of Israel ran away from the battlefield.

The men of Israel brought David to their city and chose him for their king.

David set up his home in the city of Jerusalem. There he made everything ready to welcome God. He told Zadok and the other priests to bring the Ark to Jerusalem. He remembered that wherever the Ark had travelled with the Israelites in the desert God had been with his people. David wanted God to be with them as he had been with them on the journey out of Egypt.

As the Ark came near the city gates David went out with all his people to meet the Lord. The crowds played gay songs on tambourines and trumpets and David danced all the way along the streets, leaping in the air because God was coming. As the cheerful procession passed the royal palace David's wife looked out of the window. She was very shocked to see king David dancing with the crowd in the streets.

When David came home that night his wife told him that the king should not dance with the common people. David was not ashamed of himself. "When God comes," he told her, "there is only one thing to do. Everyone should dance together."

God was pleased with David. He sent the old prophet Nathan to tell David that he would always look after him and his family. "Look at those farms where the sheep are grazing in the fields, and those little villages among the hills, and this great city of Jerusalem. The Lord has given you all these," said Nathan. "And he has given me this message for you. This is the land for my people and you are the king for my people. Your son will be king after you and his son after him. The Lord will take care of your family as long as they serve him. God will be a father to you and you will be his son."

David was very happy. He knew that God would protect his family for ever.

David did not know, as we now know, that one day a boy would be born in his family who would be God's Son.

David knew that his family would always reign over Jerusalem but he was not always pleased with life. His children were a great nuisance. They quarrelled with each other. When they grew up they quarrelled with him.

One quarrel ended in the murder of a prince at a harvest feast, another led to civil war in Israel, and towards the end of David's reign another nearly spoiled all his work. Prince Adonijah wanted very much to be king when David died. He invited the important men of Jerusalem to supper parties in his house. They liked going to parties. They agreed that he should be their next king.

David wanted prince Solomon to be king. He sent for his trusted friends, Nathan the old prophet and Zadok the priest who had brought the Ark to Jerusalem. "Take my son Solomon," he said, "to the water spring outside the city walls and crown him there as king of this people before I die."

Nathan and Zadok made Solomon king and put him on the royal donkey. As he came into Jerusalem the royal bodyguard blew their trumpets, the people shouted: "Hurrah for the son of David," and Adonijah, looking out of his window, knew that he had failed.

Solomon decided that he would build a great Temple as a house for the Ark of God. He wrote to Hiram the king of Tyre in the north, asking him to trade wood for oil and wheat. Hiram agreed and sent many cedar and juniper logs down to Jerusalem. Then Solomon organized the men of his kingdom into gangs of workmen and forced them to work without pay on the great building. While they set up the huge wooden pillars and hauled the heavy stones into place the men grumbled to one another.

In the house of the Lord Solomon placed the Ark that his father had brought to Jerusalem. All the Israelites knew that wherever the Ark was, there God was among his people. They knew that since the Ark was in the new Temple they should now come to the Temple to talk with God.

On the day that the Temple was ready Solomon ordered a grand celebration. The kir[g]
himself spoke the great prayer to God. He stood at the altar where the flame and smok[e]
went up to heaven and asked God to come to his new home in Jerusalem.

Solomon reminded the people that God had promised to look after the family [of]
David and all the people of Israel. He told the crowd standing round the altar: "God ha[s]
brought our people out of Egypt where the Israelites were slaves and has given us th[is]
land and now he has come to live in this house to show us that he is still with his peopl[e.]
We must never forget how good God has been to us. He will always be good to u[s.]
Therefore let us serve him."

The people promised to be the loyal servants of the Lord.

Solomon became very rich and powerful, and he forgot God. He thought only of his own great glory, and he forgot to look after his people. He set foremen over them and forced them to build a thick wall round the royal fortress in Jerusalem. The people grumbled.

One of the foremen was a young man called Jeroboam. As he walked from his work one afternoon he met a prophet. The prophet said to him: "Do you see this new coat of mine? Watch me tear it into twelve pieces."

"What are you doing that for?" asked Jeroboam.

"The twelve pieces are the twelve tribes of our nation," said the prophet, handing ten pieces to Jeroboam, "and you will be king of ten while Solomon's son will have only two."

Jeroboam knew that he would be killed if Solomon heard about this talk. He went into Egypt and stayed there until his chance should come.

Solomon died and his son Rehoboam came to the leaders of the tribes and said: "My father was not nearly so cruel to you as I shall be."

"Then," said the leaders of ten of the tribes from the North, "we will not choose you for our king."

Rehoboam rode away with the men of only two of the tribes. The northern tribesmen sent for Jeroboam. He came and they made him king of their ten tribes.